PORTRAIT OF

PERTH

JIRI & MARIE LOCHMAN

NEW
HOLLAND

INTRODUCTION

Freshness, vitality, dynamism and a vision for a bright future are all characteristics of Perth, the capital of Australia's largest state, Western Australia. It is a city where the future, rather than the past, is foremost on the minds of its people.

Today's population of 1.2 million is a far cry from the city's humble beginnings when Captain James Stirling arrived with a handful of settlers in 1829 to establish a new colony on the banks of the Swan River. This beautiful river is still at the heart of the city, which has its modern business centre on the north shore. The river and the city are a picturesque sight from Mount Eliza, part of Kings Park. This covers more than 400 hectares of mostly natural bushland set aside, with great foresight, as public open space in 1872.

In the northern part of the city is the Perth Cultural Centre, together with the Museum, Library and Art Gallery. While the city is at its best during the day, the night belongs to neighbouring Northbridge, with its nightclubs, cafes and restaurants.

Other places of interest can be found along the shores of the Swan River. The University of Western Australia, with its Romanesque architecture, is the oldest university in the state, established at the beginning of this century. Perth boasts five universities, giving opportunities to many young Australians, as well as a number of overseas students.

Across the river by ferry to its southern shore is the popular destination of Perth Zoo. After leaving the zoo in the late afternoon, one can take a relaxing walk along the river, with delightful views of the city skyline.

The Swan River can be followed even further downstream, right to the port of Fremantle. Here the river finally flows into the Indian Ocean, with long white sandy beaches stretching north and south of the river mouth. Fremantle was named after Captain Charles Howe Fremantle who, in 1829, formally took possession of the colony for the British Crown. The town's history can be followed through its many beautifully restored buildings. Today, Fremantle is a buzzing town where multiculturalism is alive and well. Many migrants, mainly Italians, Greeks, Chinese and Britons, help to give it its special ambience. Fremantle's trade activities are centred around the port facilities that are used for shipping the main West Australian exports of alumina, petroleum, wool and wheat.

Further west from Fremantle, just 20 kilometres away by ferry, is Rottnest Island. It was actually here that Dutchman Willem de Vlamingh landed in 1697 and became the first European to see quokkas, little wallabies that he mistook for large rats and after whom he named the island. Rottnest's main attractions, apart from quokkas, are pristine beaches with adjacent reefs that offer good diving and snorkelling.

Visitors to Perth can enjoy not only a clean, modern city, but also friendly people and a relaxed atmosphere. It's no wonder that more and more people are discovering its many attractions.

Previous pages: A panoramic view of the city of Perth and the Swan River, seen across the freeway interchange.

Above: The old Wesley Church in William Street complements the modern architecture of the central city.

Opposite: Skyscrapers in Perth's central business district tower high above the Swan River.

Above: The sun's first rays touch the city and Heirisson Island in the Swan River.

Right: The city skyline after sunset, viewed from King's Park Lookout,
glows with a myriad lights.

Above: Perth's unique relaxed lifestyle.

Left: Travelling by the *Decoy* paddleboat is an enjoyable way of getting to know Perth from a different angle.

Above: The Allan Green Plant Conservatory nestles in the greenery of Alf Curlewis Gardens.

Right: Inside the conservatory, glasshouse plants create a tropical feel, while through the glass visitors can see the city skyline.

Above: Western Australians love celebrating. They gather around the Swan River and in Kings Park to see the yearly fireworks.

Left: The Hay Street mall, brightened up by Christmas decorations, is a focal point for eager shoppers.

Above: The restored Murray Street buildings add colour and character to the central district.

Right: The Central Post Office at Forrest Place is decorated each year for the Christmas season.

Above: Charm and character make the newly restored King Street a popular spot both day and night.

Left: Narrow but attractive, King Street connects St George's Terrace with the northern end of the city.

Above left: London Court, with its array of specialist shops,
connects the Hay Street mall with St George's Terrace.

Above right: A winter night in London Court evokes a medieval atmosphere,
enhanced by the gate grill at the entrance.

Right: Built in pseudo-Tudor style, London Court was opened in 1937.
The astronomical clock above the gate is its main attraction.

Above left: Queens Gardens is one of the many inner city parks
enjoyed by office workers for relaxing lunchtime breaks.

Above right: Hyde Park, with its huge trees and small lakes, is an ideal oasis for reflection.

Left: Ponds overgrown by waterplants in Queens Gardens
are an important refuge for city waterbirds.

Above: These senior citizens enjoy a day out at their favourite pastime — bowling.

Right: The size of the WACA oval is best appreciated from the air.
Apart from cricket, it hosts football and rugby matches.

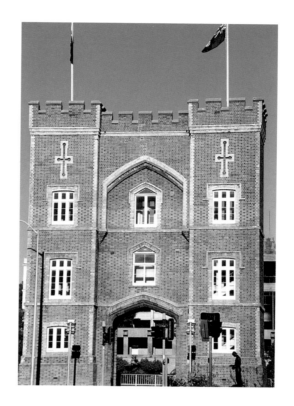

Above left: The Barracks Arch was preserved as a historical monument when the Pensioner Guard Barracks were demolished in 1966.

Above right: The Town Hall, built in 1870 with the help of convicts, is one of Perth's oldest buildings.

Left: Perth Mint, opened in 1899, still produces a wide variety of coins that are collectors' items the world over.

Above left: The old Fire Station on Murray Street is now used
as an education centre and museum.

Above right: The beautifully refurbished His Majesty's Theatre enjoys
a significant position in the cultural scene of Perth.

Right: The Palace Hotel, restored to its former splendour, is now part
of the modern complex of Bank West.

Above: The redevelopment of the old Swan Brewery has caused a controversy between Aboriginal people and the State Government over land rights.

Left: The brewery, located on Mounts Bay Road, enjoys an idyllic position at the foot of Mount Eliza.

34   Above: The Perth Observatory began its life in 1875 as a meteorological station on the high ground opposite Kings Park.

Above: Government House, completed in 1864, has retained its status as an important landmark of the city.

Above: Mediterranean Romanesque architecture is characteristic of Winthrop Hall.

Left: Winthrop Hall and its clocktower overlook the gardens and lecture halls at the University of Western Australia.

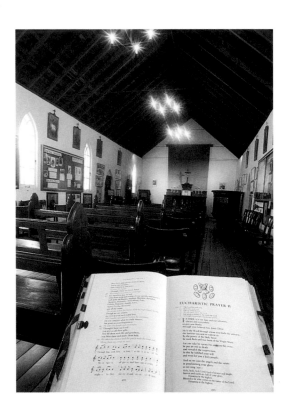

Above left: St Mary's Roman Catholic Cathedral, built in 1865,
is a major feature of Victoria Square.

Above right: The serene interior of St John's Protestant Cathedral invites
visitors to enjoy a few moments of quiet contemplation.

Right: St George's Anglican Cathedral, erected from 1879 to 1888, stands slightly
to the east of where the original Anglican church of St George once stood.

Above left: An avenue of lemon-scented gums leads to lookouts at Kings Park.

Above right: The War Memorial overlooks the Swan River and the city from Mount Eliza.

Left: In 1901, the area around Mount Eliza, a popular meeting place since 1872, was named Kings Park.

42   Above: The striking red and green colours of the native kangaroo paw contrast sharply with a white smokebush.

Above: Every spring, the wildflower gardens of Kings Park are transformed into a blaze of colour.

Above: The flower display at the Kings Park Wildflower Clock changes every year.

Top: Old cannons standing among flowerbeds are a vivid reminder of the past.

Right: Tram coaches are a favourite with tourists.

Following pages: The Sheraton Hotel on Adelaide Terrace is a clearly recognisable landmark from the southern shore of the Swan River.

Above: The Horseshoe Bridge was completed in 1904 and its architecture reflects the style of that period.

Opposite: The bridge connects Perth city with a variety of restaurants and night life in Northbridge.

Above: Dining in street cafes such as the Cafe Villa on Oxford Street is a popular pastime on hot summer nights.

Above: Northbridge is the focal point of city nightlife with the brightly lit Brass Monkey Hotel enticing people to the area.

Above left: The newly opened Subiaco shopping complex attracts
more people from the city to the suburbs.

Above right: One of the best known theatres in Perth is the Regal Theatre in the heart of Subiaco.

Right: The Subiaco Hotel at the crossroads of Hay Street and Rokeby
Road is the focus of evening entertainment.

Above: An aerial view of Barrack Street Jetty shows ferries lined up for their daily journeys on the river.

Above: People waiting for boat cruises and ferries pass their time at Moorings Cafe at the Old Perth Port.

Above: The walking path along Riverside Drive is favoured by early morning and lunchtime joggers.

Opposite: Stately palm trees form a line between the Swan River and busy Riverside Drive.

Following pages: The Narrows Bridge spans the Swan River, allowing the traffic to flow freely from north to south.

Above: The South Perth Esplanade offers magnificent views of the city skyline.

Left: Lit by the setting sun and thousands of man-made lights, the Narrows Bridge and Perth cityscape create a multihued image.

Following pages: Early morning mist on the Swan River takes the viewer back in time to when the modern, busy city centre was only a dream.

Above: The Black Swan, emblem of Western Australia, can be seen
on numerous city lakes and at Perth Zoo.

Top: This small tour train takes visitors through the most important exhibits of the zoo.

Left: A modern restaurant and cafeteria are set among palm trees and chattering birds.

Above: The Old Mill in South Perth boasts a collection of authentic horse-drawn carriages.

Right: The Old Mill and Miller's Cottage are remnants of the original settlers' architecture of the 1830s.

Above: Burswood Park on the Swan River foreshore invites a pleasant
stroll past an impressive collection of sculptures.

Left: The lavish setting of the Burswood Resort Hotel and Casino stands
as proof of the contemporary prosperity of the state.

Following pages: Blue waters, white sand and sunshine await visitors to the West Coast.

Above: The Indiana Tea House at Cottlesloe Beach offers refreshment to beach goers.

Top: The Surf Lifesaving Club rooms dominate sun-drenched and crowded Cottlesloe Beach.

Left: The Cottesloe Hotel on the ocean front draws crowds for a refreshing cold drink after a long, hot day.

Above: Hundreds of water sports enthusiasts are attracted to the Trigg Surf Carnival each year.

Top: A number of excellent restaurants and cafes dot the beaches of the northern suburbs.

Right: Young surfers or 'grommits' take advantage of good surfing conditions at Trigg Beach.

Above: Women surf life-savers complete their training session at Scarborough Beach.

Top: Western Australia is renowned for its good surf, and surfing
is consequently one of the most popular sports in the state.

Left: Balmy summer afternoons can be whiled away at a range of Scarborough cafes.

Following pages: Sunrise over Matilda Bay jetty reveals the city silhouetted in the distance.

Above: Anchored yachts at yacht club jetties are a distinctive feature of the Swan River.

Above: The boat-packed Hillary's Boat Harbour is proof that Western Australia is a state of ocean lovers.

Above: An aerial view of the Claremont Yacht Club nestled in a quiet bend of the Swan River known as Freshwater Bay.

Top: Green bushland adorns the river foreshore at the peaceful Armstrong Spit.

Right: Boats bob tranquilly on the river at Mosman Bay.

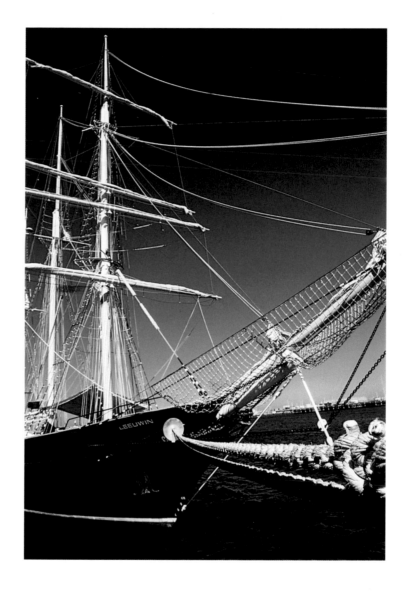

Above: The sail training ship *Leeuwin*, anchored in Fremantle Harbour.

Left: Success Boat Harbour in Fremantle was built for the America's Cup in 1987.

Above: Fremantle Port, completed under the supervision of the colony's chief engineer in 1897, took only five years to build.

Above: The port of Fremantle is a vital lifeline for Western Australian trade. It handles about 50 per cent of the state's imports and exports.

Above left and above right: Every weekend shoppers looking for a bargain
flock to the Fremantle Markets.

Right: South Terrace, where the young and old of Fremantle meet over
a cup of coffee, is known locally as the 'Cappuccino Strip'.

Above: Street cafes create a pleasant Mediterranean atmosphere in the heart of Fremantle.

Left: As night falls, people desert South Terrace. However, they will return
later in the evening for a night of entertainment.

Above: This shellfish float is just one of the mysterious contraptions forming part of the Lotteries Parade at the Festival.

Right: Every year in summer the streets come alive with colour, music and laughter at the Fremantle Festival.

Above: Cicerello's Fish Market is a favourite venue for those who like eating their lunch of fresh fish by the ocean.

Opposite: The trendy Left Bank tavern on the Swan River is ideal for watching river traffic over a drink.

Above left and left: The Fremantle Prison, today a museum,
was the first of many buildings built by convicts.

Above right: The most cherished exhibit of the Fremantle Maritime Museum
is the 1629 wreck of the *Batavia*.

Above: The twelve-sided building known as the Round House was the first civil prison of the colony.

Above: Visitors inspect the well in the centre of the Round House courtyard, built in 1831.

Above: The crucifix in the school yard of the independent Guildford Anglican Grammar School.

Opposite: Woodbridge House, built in the Victorian style, is a reminder of Guildford as it was in the 1890s.

Above: The interior of the Anglican Grammar School chapel
is highlighted by a narrow strip of sunlight.

Right: The chapel is a centrepiece of the Guildford
Historic Centre, the first settlement east of Perth.

Above left: Signs at the newly established Joondalup Central Park attempt to increase the environmental awareness of the visitors.

Above right: Canoeists enjoy a foggy dawn at Lake Joondalup, an important wetland area nestled among the northern suburbs.

Left: Joondalup, a modern city in the 'northern corridor' of Perth, is one of the fastest growing areas in Australia.

Above: This historic tunnel, once part of the railway line connecting Fremantle and York, is now in the John Forrest National Park.

Right: After the first rains, the Jane Brook in John Forrest National Park cascades down the Darling Range escarpment with renewed vigour.

Above: The Mundaring Dam was completed in 1903. It supplies water to the goldfields, 560 kilometres away.

Opposite: The Darling Range above the Swan River Basin is timbered with jarrah,
stands of which pierce the morning mist.

Above: Koalas kept at Yanchep National Park, just an hour's drive north
of the city, draw crowds of admirers to their enclosure.

Right: Bird-spotting tour boats take visitors on a cruise
of Loch McNess in the centre of the park.

Above: York's attractive town hall, built in 1911, is testimony to the town's prosperity as the agricultural centre of the Avon valley.

Above: In Toodyay, the historical court house is currently used as the Shire Office.

Above: Visitors can marvel at the display of old farm tools at Katrine, near Toodyay.

Top: The Old Newcastle gaol, presently a museum, was built in 1865.
The town of Newcastle is now called Toodyay.

Right: Katrine, where this historic barn stands, flourished before the railway
to Northam was constructed.

Above: Fishing fever is apparent on the Old Mandurah Bridge,
especially when the prawns are running from Peel Inlet to the ocean.

Top: The Mandurah canal development brought luxury lifestyle accommodation to the area.

Left: The Peel Inlet, the largest pelican breeding ground in Western Australia,
is sure to impress any visitor to Mandurah.

Above: Wildlife cruises take tourists to Seal Island to view the resident Australian sea-lions.

Right: Rocky shores at Penguin Island, off Rockingham, are home to a colony of Little Penguins.

Above: New arrivals flood the Visitor Centre seeking information about Rottnest Island.

Top: The quokka is familiar to all visitors to Rottnest Island. It can be seen at night hopping along the streets.

Left: Sunrise at Thomson Bay gives a soft glow to the houses on the shore.

Perth

Above: Rottnest Island is renowned for its hidden, quiet bays like Eagle Bay,
viewed here through a natural bridge.

Top: The tourist train puffs up from the main settlement to Oliver Hill at the centre of the island.

Right: A stretch of sandy beach and a calm ocean summon beach goers
for a swim or snorkel on the reef.

Above: Bathurst Point Lighthouse, near Geordie Bay,
is a landmark on the eastern side of the island.

Left: Geordie Bay, with its comfortable seaside accommodation
and safe anchorage, is favoured by boat owners.

Above: Rottnest Island is an ideal holiday location for people who love water sports.

Right: The clarity of the water attracts divers who come on their boats to explore the reefs.

First published in Australia in 1998 by
New Holland Publishers (Australia) Pty Ltd
Sydney • Auckland • London • Cape Town

14 Aquatic Drive, Frenchs Forest, NSW 2086, Australia
1A/218 Lake Road, Northcote, Auckland, New Zealand
24 Nutford Place, London W1H 6DQ, United Kingdom
80 McKenzie Street, Cape Town 8001, South Africa

PHOTOGRAPHIC ACKNOWLEDGEMENTS

Abbreviations: LT = Lochman Transparencies
Photographic Positions: l = left, r = right, t= top, b = bottom
Bill Belson/LT: pp. 4, 12, 19, 22r,36, 40, 41r, 44t, 49, 50, 51, 52l&r, 53, 55, 60, 72, 73t&b, 88r, 94, 96, 97l, 128;
Eva Boogard/LT: p. 105r; **Mike Braham/LT:** pp. 15, 25l, 64, 65t, 66, 67, 88l; **Brian Downs/LT:** pp. 23, 62–63; **John Kleczkowski/LT:** pp. 87, 90, 92, 93, 109; **Jiri Lochman/LT:** pp. 1, 5, 6–7, 11, 24, 27, 58–59, 65b, 77t, 81, 84, 86, 98, 102, 103, 108, 100, 101, 111, 112, 113, 114t&b, 115, 116, 117t&b, 118, 121t&b, 122t&b, 125, 126; **Marie Lochman/LT:** pp. 10, 46–47, 54, 82t&b, 107, 120, 123, 124, 127; **Dennis Sarson/LT:** pp. 9, 13, 22l, 25r, 26, 30l, 34, 35, 37, 38l&r, 41l, 44b, 56, 68, 74t&b, 75, 76, 78–79, 80, 83, 89, 95, 99, 104, 106, 110; **Len Stewart/LT:** pp. 8, 14, 16, 17, 18, 20, 21, 28, 29l&r, 30r, 31, 32, 33, 39, 42, 43, 45, 48, 57, 61, 69, 70–71, 77b, 85, 91, 97r, 105l, 119.

National Library of Australia Cataloguing-in-Publication Data:
    Lochman, Jiri.
    Portrait of Perth.

    ISBN 1 86436 374 6

    1. Perth (W.A.) – Description and travel.
    2. Perth (W.A.) – Pictorial works.
    919.411

Publishing General Manager: Jane Hazell
Publisher: Averill Chase
Editors: Anouska Good, Joanna Munnelly
Designer: Peta Nugent
Picture Research: Bronwyn Rennex, Raquel Hill
Reproduction by DNL Resources
Printed and bound by Times Publishing Group, Malaysia

Half title photograph: Black swans with cygnets
Title page photograph: Cafe Villa in Northbridge
Page 4: Cottesloe Beach
Page 5: Kangaroo paw
This page: Old Perth Port